Summary

Immigration policy in the United States reflects multiple goals. First, it serves to reunite families by admitting immigrants who already have family members living in the United States. Second, it seeks to admit workers with specific skills and to fill positions in occupations deemed to be experiencing labor shortages. Third, it attempts to provide a refuge for people who face the risk of political, racial, or religious persecution in their country of origin. Finally, it seeks to ensure diversity by providing admission to people from countries with historically low rates of immigration to the United States. Several categories of permanent and temporary admission have been established to implement those wide-ranging goals.

This Congressional Budget Office paper describes who is eligible for the various categories of legal admission and provides the most recent data available about the number of people admitted under each category. The paper also discusses procedures currently used to enforce immigration laws and provides estimates of the number of people who are in the United States illegally.

Lawful Entry

U.S. policy provides two distinct paths for the lawful admission of noncitizens, or "aliens": permanent (immigrant) admission or temporary (nonimmigrant) admission. In the first category, aliens may be granted permanent admission by being accorded the status of lawful permanent residents (LPRs). Aliens admitted in such a capacity are formally classified as "immigrants" and receive a permanent resident card, commonly referred to as a green card. Lawful permanent residents are eligible to work in the United States and may later apply for U.S. citizenship.

In 2004, the United States granted permanent admission, or LPR status, to about 946,000 noncitizens (see Summary Table 1). That figure is not a measure of first-time entries into the United States, however. The U.S. Citizenship and Immigration Services—a bureau of the Department of Homeland Security—counts both entries of new immigrants and adjustments to lawful permanent resident status (for those aliens already in the United States) as "admissions." In 2004, roughly 584,000 adjustments to LPR status were granted, and about 362,000 new immigrants entered the country.

The second path is admission on a temporary basis. Temporary admission encompasses a large and diverse group of people who are granted entry to the United States for a specific purpose for a limited period of time. Reasons for such admissions include tourism, diplomatic missions, study, and temporary work. Under U.S. law, citizens of foreign countries admitted temporarily are classified as "nonimmigrants." (For definitions of terms used in this paper, see Box 1 on page 3.) Certain nonimmigrants may be permitted to work in the United States for a limited time depending on the type of visa they receive. However, they are not eligible for citizenship through naturalization; nonimmigrants wishing to remain in the United States on a permanent basis must apply for permanent admission.

In 2004, the State Department issued about 5 million visas authorizing temporary admission to the United States, according to preliminary data. In addition, under the Visa Waiver Program, 15.8 million people were admitted that year on a temporary basis. Under that program, eligible people may enter the United States without a visa for business or pleasure visits of 90 days or less.

The numbers presented in this paper indicate the flow of noncitizens into the United States but not their departure. Such information is not recorded. Official estimates are available only on the departures of lawful permanent residents. The Bureau of the Census has estimated that an average of 217,000 LPRs emigrated from the United States each year between 1990 and 2000.

Summary Table 1.

Lawful Admissions and Issuances of Visas, 2000 to 2004

(Thousands)

	2000	2001	2002	2003	2004
	Permanent (Immigrant) Admissions				
Admissions of Lawful Permanent Residents[a]					
Unrestricted					
Immediate Relatives of U.S. Citizens	348	443	486	333	406
Generally restricted					
Family-sponsored preference admissions	235	232	187	159	214
Employment-sponsored preference admissions	107	179	175	82	155
Refugees and asylum-seekers[b]	66	109	126	45	71
Diversity admissions	51	42	43	46	50
Other	43	59	47	41	49
Total	**850**	**1,064**	**1,064**	**706**	**946**
	Temporary (Nonimmigrant) Admissions and Issuances				
Visa Issuances[c]	7,142	7,589	5,769	4,882	5,049[d]
Admissions Under the Visa Waiver Program (Includes multiple entries)[e]	17,595	16,471	13,113	13,490	15,762

Source: Congressional Budget Office based on Department of Justice, Immigration and Naturalization Service, *2001 Statistical Yearbook of the Immigration and Naturalization Service* (February 2003); Department of Homeland Security, Office of Immigration Statistics, *2003 Yearbook of Immigration Statistics* (September 2004) and *2004 Yearbook of Immigration Statistics* (January 2006); and Department of State, Bureau of Consular Affairs, *Report of the Visa Office 2003*, available at http://travel.state.gov/visa/about/report/report_2750.html.

a. This category includes both those aliens who entered the United States as lawful permanent residents (LPRs) and those already present in the country who adjusted to LPR status in the year designated.

b. Refugees and asylum-seekers are people who are unable or unwilling to return to their home country because of the risk of persecution or because of a well-founded fear of persecution. Refugees apply for admission from outside of the United States; asylum-seekers request legal admission from within the United States or at a U.S. port of entry.

c. Because certain visas allow nonimmigrants to enter the United States within a window of a few years, the year of issuance might not reflect an alien's actual year of entry. Furthermore, Canadians who travel to the United States on business or as tourists on a short-term basis generally do not need a visa, nor do eligible citizens from countries participating in the Visa Waiver Program.

d. According to preliminary data from the Department of State.

e. The Visa Waiver Program allows eligible citizens of 27 participating countries to enter the United States without a visa for visits of 90 days or less that are related to business or tourism. The participating countries are Andorra, Australia, Austria, Belgium, Brunei, Denmark, Finland, France, Germany, Iceland, Ireland, Italy, Japan, Liechtenstein, Luxembourg, Monaco, the Netherlands, New Zealand, Norway, Portugal, San Marino, Singapore, Slovenia, Spain, Sweden, Switzerland, and the United Kingdom. In recording nonimmigrant admissions, multiple entries by the same individual are not distinguished from first-time entries; therefore, the figures provided do not accurately represent the yearly flow of new nonimmigrants to the United States under this program.

Unlawful Entry

In addition to facilitating the lawful admission of both immigrants and nonimmigrants, U.S. policy addresses the issue of unauthorized aliens in the United States. According to the Census Bureau and the former Immigration and Naturalization Service, about 7 million unauthorized aliens were in the United States in 2000. Other researchers have estimated that number at roughly 10 million in early 2004. Although such estimates convey the population of unauthorized aliens living in the United States in a given year, the other statistics presented in this paper represent annual inflows of people into the United States, unless otherwise indicated.

Aliens found to be in violation of U.S. immigration laws may be removed from the country through a formal process (which can include penalties such as fines, imprisonment, or prohibition against future entry) or may be offered the chance to depart voluntarily (which does not preclude future entry). In 2004, about 203,000 people were formally removed, and about 1 million others departed voluntarily (some people may have done so more than once). Of the 203,000 formal removals, 42,000 unauthorized aliens were subject to expedited removals, a process designed to speed up the removal of aliens seeking to enter the country illegally.

Immigration Policy in the United States

The Evolution of U.S. Immigration Policy

Immigration has been a subject of legislation for U.S. policymakers since the nation's founding. In 1790, the Congress established a process enabling people born abroad to become U.S. citizens. The first federal law limiting immigration qualitatively was enacted in 1875, prohibiting the admission of criminals and prostitutes. The following year, in addressing efforts by the states to control immigration, the Supreme Court declared that the regulation of immigration was the exclusive responsibility of the federal government. As the number of immigrants rose, the Congress established the Immigration Service in 1891, and the federal government assumed responsibility for processing all immigrants seeking admission to the United States.

During World War I, immigration levels were relatively low. However, when mass immigration resumed after the war, quantitative restrictions were introduced. The Congress established a new immigration policy: a national-origins quota system, enacted as part of the Quota Law in 1921 and revised in 1924. Immigration was restricted by assigning each nationality a quota based on its representation in past U.S. census figures. The Department of State distributed a limited number of visas each year through U.S. embassies abroad, and the Immigration Service admitted immigrants who arrived with a valid visa. Citizens of other countries could move permanently to the United States by applying for an immigrant visa. Foreign citizens traveling to the United States for a limited time (for instance, foreign exchange students, business executives, or tourists) could apply for a nonimmigrant visa.

Family reunification was a fundamental goal of the Quota Law of 1921 and the updated quota law of 1924. Those laws favored immediate relatives of U.S. citizens and other family members, either by exempting them from numerical restrictions or by granting them preference within the restrictions. Subsequent laws continued to focus on family reunification as a major goal of immigration policy.

The Immigration and Nationality Act Amendments of 1965 abolished the national-origins quota system and established a categorical preference system. The new system provided preferences for relatives of U.S. citizens and lawful permanent residents and for immigrants with job skills deemed useful to the United States. However, it did not abolish numerical restrictions altogether. For countries in the Eastern Hemisphere (comprising Europe, Asia, Africa, and Australia), the amendments set per-country and total immigration caps, as well as a cap for each of the preference categories. Although there was a total cap established on immigration from the Western Hemisphere, neither the preference categories nor per-country limits were applied to immigrants from the Western Hemisphere. Immediate relatives of U.S. citizens—spouses, children under 21, and parents of citizens over 21—were exempted from the caps.

The policies established in the 1965 amendments are still largely in place, although they have been modified at various times. In 1976, the categorical preference system was extended to applicants from the Western Hemisphere. In 1978, the numerical restrictions for Eastern and Western Hemisphere immigration were combined into a single annual worldwide ceiling of 290,000. The Immigration Act of 1990 added a category of admission based on diversity and increased the worldwide immigration ceiling to the current "flexible" cap of 675,000 per year. That cap can exceed 675,000 in any year when unused visas from the family-sponsored and employment-based categories are available from the previous year. For example, if only 625,000 people were admitted in 2006, the cap would then be raised to 725,000 for 2007.

The United States also has participated in the resettlement of specific groups of refugees since the close of World War II. The Refugee Act of 1980 created a comprehensive refugee policy giving the President, in consultation with the Congress, the authority to determine the number of refugees that would be admitted on a yearly basis. It brought U.S. policy in line with the 1967 Protocol to the 1951 United Nations Refugee Convention. The protocol, together with the 1969 Organization of African Unity Convention, expanded the number of people considered refugees. The Refugee Act adopted the internationally accepted definition of "refugee" contained in the U.N. Convention and Protocol Relating to the Status of Refugees and applied the same definition to those seeking asylum.

The Immigration Reform and Control Act of 1986 addressed the issue of unauthorized immigration. It sought to enhance enforcement and to create new pathways to legal immigration. Sanctions were imposed on employers who knowingly hired or recruited unauthorized aliens. The law also created two amnesty programs for unauthorized aliens and a new classification for seasonal agricultural workers. The Seasonal Agricultural Worker amnesty program allowed people who had worked for at least 90 days in certain agricultural jobs to apply for permanent resident status. The Legally Authorized Workers amnesty program allowed current unauthorized aliens who had lived in the United States since 1982 to legalize their status. Under the two amnesty programs, roughly 2.7 million people residing in the United States illegally became lawful permanent residents.[1]

In response to continuing concerns about unauthorized immigration, the Illegal Immigration Reform and Immigrant Responsibility Act of 1996 addressed border enforcement and the use of social services by immigrants. It increased the number of border patrol agents, introduced new border control measures, reduced government benefits available to immigrants, and established a pilot program in which employers and social services agencies could check by telephone or electronically to verify the eligibility of immigrants applying for work or social services benefits.[2]

The Homeland Security Act of 2002 created the Department of Homeland Security (DHS) and, in doing so, restructured the Immigration and Naturalization Service (INS), the agency formerly responsible for immigration services, border enforcement, and border inspections. Nearly all functions of the INS were transferred to DHS. Prior law had combined immigrant service and enforcement functions within the same agency; those functions are now divided among different bureaus of DHS. Immigration and naturalization are the responsibility of the Bureau of Citizenship and Immigration Services. The border enforcement functions of the INS are split between two bureaus: the Bureau of Customs and Border Protection and the Bureau of Immigration and Customs Enforcement.

Categories of Lawful Admission to the United States

Current immigration policy offers two distinct ways for noncitizens to enter the United States lawfully: permanent (or immigrant) admission and temporary (or nonimmigrant) admission. People granted permanent admission are formally classified as lawful permanent residents (LPRs) and receive a green card. (The term "immigrant" is correctly applied only to that category of aliens. For more definitions of terms used in this paper, see Box 1.) LPRs are eligible to work in the United States and eventually may apply for U.S. citizenship.[3] Aliens eligible for permanent admission include certain relatives of U.S. citizens and workers with specific job skills, among others. In 2004, the United States admitted about 946,000 people as lawful permanent residents.

---

1. Nancy Rytina, "IRCA Legalization Effects: Lawful Permanent Residence and Naturalization through 2001" (paper presented at The Effects of Immigrant Legalization Programs on the United States: Scientific Evidence on Immigrant Adaptation and Impact on U.S. Economy and Society, The Cloister, Mary Woodward Lasker Center, National Institutes of Health Main Campus, October 25, 2002).

2. The employment verification pilot program is voluntary, and the Government Accountability Office has found weaknesses in it. See Government Accountability Office, *Immigration Enforcement: Weaknesses Hinder Employment Verification and Worksite Enforcement Efforts*, GAO-05-813 (August 2005).

3. The naturalization process and requirements for citizenship are described in the appendix.

Box 1.

Definition of Terms

Terminology used throughout this paper is defined by the Department of Homeland Security's Bureau of Citizenship and Immigration Services:

■ **Alien** refers to any individual who is not a citizen of the United States.

■ **Immigrant** refers to an alien lawfully admitted to the United States for permanent residence; such people also may be referred to as **lawful permanent residents**.

■ **Nonimmigrant** refers to an alien who seeks temporary entry to the United States for a specific purpose. Nonimmigrants include tourists, temporary workers, business executives, students, and diplomats.

■ **Removal** is the expulsion of an alien from the United States. The expulsion may be based on grounds of inadmissibility or deportability.

■ A U.S. **visa** allows the bearer to apply for entry to the United States under a certain classification. Examples of classifications include student (F), visitor (B), and temporary worker (H). A visa does not grant the bearer the right to enter the United States. The Department of State is responsible for visa adjudication at U.S. embassies and consulates outside of the United States. Immigration inspectors with the Department of Homeland Security's Bureau of Customs and Border Protection determine admission into the United States at a port of entry, as well as the duration and conditions of stay.

The 946,000 new admissions reported for 2004 include more than first-time entries into the United States. The U.S. Citizenship and Immigration Services (USCIS) counts as "admissions" both new entries of immigrants and adjustments to LPR status for aliens already in the United States. In 2004, for example, roughly 584,000 adjustments to LPR status were granted and about 362,000 aliens entered the country for the first time (see Table 1).

The second path to lawful admission is temporary admission, which is granted to foreign citizens who seek entry to the United States for a limited time and for a specific purpose (such as tourism, diplomacy, temporary work, or study). Under U.S. law, aliens admitted on a temporary basis are classified as "nonimmigrants." Only nonimmigrants with a specific type of visa may be permitted to work in the United States. Nonimmigrants are not eligible for citizenship through naturalization; those wishing to remain in the United States permanently must apply for permanent admission. In 2004, about 5 million people were granted visas for temporary admission.

Annual issuances of temporary visas, however, are not a measure of the number of nonimmigrants entering the country each year. Most temporary visas are valid for several years after they are issued. Thus, issuance and entry may occur in different years, and visa holders may enter the country multiple times. The USCIS does report annual admissions for nonimmigrants, but those numbers measure entries by nonimmigrants, not just first-time entries. For example, each entry by a foreign exchange student returning from his or her home country after school holidays is counted as an admission. Neither yearly temporary visa issuances nor yearly temporary admissions can be directly compared with the measure of yearly permanent admissions.

It is important to note that the numbers presented throughout this paper indicate flows of noncitizens into the United States but not their departures. Information on departures of noncitizens from the United States is not recorded, and official estimates are available only on the departures of lawful permanent residents. An earlier paper by the Congressional Budget Office found that the best estimates indicate that one-fourth to one-third of legal immigrants leave the United States, in most cases within several years of admission.[4] The Census Bureau

---

4. See Congressional Budget Office, *A Description of the Immigrant Population* (November 2004); and Tammany J. Mulder, Betsy Guzmán, and Angela Brittingham, *Evaluating Components of International Migration: Foreign-Born Emigrants*, Population Division Working Paper No. 62 (Department of Commerce, Bureau of the Census, April 2002), p. 6, available at www.census.gov/population/www/techpap.html.

Table 1.

Permanent (Immigrant) Admissions, by Category of New Arrival, 1996 to 2004

	1996	1997	1998	1999	2000	2001	2002	2003	2004
Number of New Admissions, by Type									
First-time entry to the United States	421,405	380,719	357,037	401,775	407,402	411,059	384,427	358,411	362,221
Adjustment of status to LPR	494,495	417,659	297,414	244,793	442,405	653,259	679,305	347,416	583,921
Total	**915,900**	**798,378**	**654,451**	**646,568**	**849,807**	**1,064,318**	**1,063,732**	**705,827**	**946,142**
Percentage of New Admissions, by Type									
First-time entry to the United States	46	48	55	62	48	39	36	51	38
Adjustment of status to LPR	54	52	45	38	52	61	64	49	62

Source: Congressional Budget Office based on Department of Homeland Security, Office of Immigration Statistics, *2004 Yearbook of Immigration Statistics* (January 2006).

Note: LPR = lawful permanent resident.

has estimated that between 1990 and 2000, an average of 217,000 foreign-born people left the United States annually.[5]

Under certain conditions, the United States may deny visas or admission on either a temporary or a permanent basis. For example, people may be denied admission on the grounds of health, criminal history, security or terrorism concerns, the likelihood of their "becoming a public charge," their seeking work in the United States without proper labor certification and qualifications, prior illegal entry or violations of immigration law, lack of proper documentation, or previous removal from the country. Those grounds may be waived for certain admission categories.

It is difficult to determine how many people might seek to enter the United States, on either a permanent or temporary basis. Various factors in addition to numerical limits affect those admissions. For example, backlogs in the processing of applications for visas for permanent legal residency and for nonimmigrant visas may slow admissions for the year. Waiting periods may vary by country and deter people who would otherwise seek lawful entry to the United States.

5. Tammany J. Mulder and others, *U.S. Census Bureau Measurement of Net International Migration to the United States: 1990 to 2000*, Population Division Working Paper No. 51 (Department of Commerce, Bureau of the Census, December 2001), available at www.census.gov/population/www/techpap.html.

Permanent Admission

The goals of current immigration policy are wide-ranging:

■ To reunite families by admitting immigrants who already have family members living in the United States;

■ To admit workers in occupations with strong demand for labor;

■ To provide a refuge for people who face the risk of political, racial, or religious persecution in their home countries; and

■ To provide admission to people from a diverse set of countries.

Several categories of permanent admission have been established to implement those goals.

Admissions of Immediate Relatives of U.S. Citizens. In keeping with the objective of family reunification, the immediate relatives of U.S. citizens—spouses, parents of citizens ages 21 and older, and unmarried children under 21—are admitted without numerical limitation. In 2004, about 406,000 immediate relatives of U.S. citizens were admitted, accounting for about 43 percent of all permanent admissions. Immediate relatives of citizens have generally accounted for the largest share of permanent immigrant admissions (see Figure 1).

Figure 1.

Total Lawful Permanent Admissions, by Admissions Category, 2004

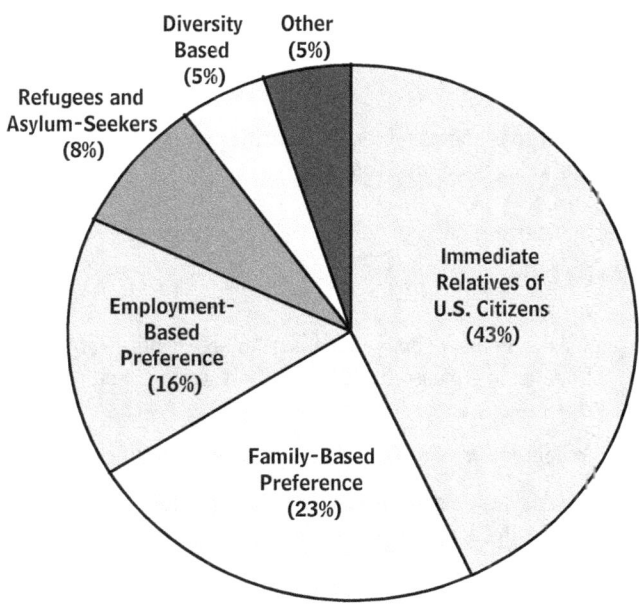

Source: Congressional Budget Office based on Department of Homeland Security, Office of Immigration Statistics, *2004 Yearbook of Immigration Statistics* (January 2006).

Note: In 2004, the latest year for which data are available, there were 946,142 permanent admissions.

Family-Sponsored Preference Admissions. In addition to their immediate relatives, U.S. citizens can sponsor other relatives for permanent admission under the family-sponsored preference program, which is subject to numerical limits. Under that program, admission is governed by a system of ordered preferences (see Table 2). In 2004, about 214,000 people—or 23 percent of all lawful permanent immigrants—were granted admission under the family-sponsored preference program. Between this category and the preceding (for immediate relatives of U.S. citizens), family-based immigrants accounted for almost two-thirds of permanent admissions in 2004.

The various preference categories under the family-sponsored program (and under the employment-based program described below) have different numerical limits (see Table 3). Unused visas in each category may be passed to the next-lower preference category, and unused visas in the lowest preference category are passed on to the first category. Actual admissions often fall short of the

established ceilings—for instance, the 214,000 people admitted in 2004 compare with a total ceiling for all family-based categories of 226,000 visas—because of either low demand for visas or processing backlogs that sometimes affect the number of admissions granted each year.

Employment-Based Preference Admissions. Historically, U.S. immigration policy also has sought to bring in workers with certain job skills. The country currently has five employment-based preference categories under which a person may be admitted:

■ Priority workers with extraordinary ability in the arts, athletics, business, education, or science;[6]

■ Professionals holding advanced degrees or individuals of exceptional ability;

■ Workers in occupations deemed to be experiencing shortages;

■ Religious and other special workers;[7] and

■ People willing to invest at least $1 million in businesses located in the United States.

A total of about 155,000 people were admitted in 2004 under those employment-based preference categories, accounting for roughly 16 percent of permanent admissions. The majority of them—55 percent—were admitted as workers in occupations deemed to be experiencing shortages (see Table 3).

For most immigrants to be admitted under the employment-based preference program, an employer must first submit a labor certification request to the Department of Labor. The department must then certify that there are not enough U.S. workers available locally to perform the intended work or that the employment of the immigrant worker will not adversely affect wages and

6.   Extraordinary ability refers to a level of expertise that indicates the individual is one of a small percentage who have risen to the very top of a particular field of endeavor. See 8 C.F.R. 204.5 for further details.

7.   Ibid. Religious workers include ministers authorized by a recognized denomination to conduct religious worship and perform duties usually performed by members of the clergy. (The category does not include lay preachers.)

Table 2.

Major Immigration Categories

Category	Who Qualifies for Category
Immediate Relatives of U.S. Citizens	Spouses and unmarried children (under 21 years of age) of U.S. citizens; parents of U.S. citizens ages 21 and older
Family-Based Immigration	
First preference	Unmarried adult (ages 21 and older) sons and daughters of U.S. citizens
Second preference	Spouses and dependent children of LPRs; unmarried sons and daughters of LPRs
Third preference	Married sons and daughters of U.S. citizens
Fourth preference	Siblings of adult U.S. citizens
Employment-Based Immigration	
First preference	Priority workers: Individuals with extraordinary ability in the arts, athletics, business, education, or the sciences; outstanding professors and researchers; certain multinational executives and managers
Second preference	Professionals who hold advanced degrees or who are considered to have exceptional ability
Third preference	Skilled workers with at least two years' training or experience in labor sectors deemed to have shortages and professionals with baccalaureate degrees; unskilled workers in labor sectors deemed to have shortages
Fourth preference	Special immigrants: Ministers, other religious workers, certain foreign nationals employed by the U.S. government abroad, and others
Fifth preference	Employment-creation investors who commit at least $1 million to the development of at least 10 new jobs. (The amount of the investment may be less for rural areas or areas of high unemployment.)

- -

Continued

working conditions in the United States. (Certification is waived for three preference categories: ministers and other religious workers, workers with extraordinary ability, and investors in U.S. businesses.) After receiving certification, the employer must file a petition with the USCIS on behalf of the immigrant.

Refugees and Asylum-Seekers. The third goal of U.S. immigration policy is to provide a haven for refugees and asylum-seekers—people who are unable or unwilling to return to their home country because of persecution (or a well-founded fear of persecution) on account of their race, religion, nationality, membership in a particular social group, or political opinions. The difference between refugees and asylum-seekers is one of location. Refugees apply for admission to the United States from outside the country, whereas aliens seeking asylum status request legal admission from within the United States or at a U.S. port of entry.

The number of refugees admitted to the United States on an annual basis and the allocation of that number between countries are determined by the President in consultation with the Congress. In practice, U.S. policy has been to allow admission of at least half of the refugees identified by the U.N. High Commissioner for Refugees as being in need of resettlement.[8] Typically, some portion of refugee admissions are unreserved (not allocated to a particular country) in an effort to meet any unexpected need for resettlement.

_____

8. Department of Health and Human Services, Department of Homeland Security, and Department of State, *Proposed Refugee Admissions for Fiscal Year 2005: Report to Congress* (September 2004), p. 2.

Table 2.

Continued

Category	Who Qualifies for Category
Refugees[a]	Aliens who have been granted refugee status in the United States because of the risk of persecution or a well-founded fear of persecution. Refugees must wait one year before petitioning for LPR status
Asylum-Seekers[a]	Aliens who have been granted asylum in the United States because of the risk of persecution or a well-founded fear of persecution. Asylum-seekers must wait one year before petitioning for LPR status
Diversity Program	Citizens of foreign nations with historically low levels of admission to the United States. To qualify for a diversity visa, an applicant must have a high school education or the equivalent, or at least two years of training or experience in an occupation
Other	Various classes of immigrants, such as Amerasians, parolees, certain Central Americans, Cubans, and Haitians adjusting to LPR status, and certain people granted LPR status following removal proceedings[b]

Source: Congressional Budget Office based on Department of Homeland Security, U.S. Citizenship and Immigration Services, "Green Cards (LPR)," available at http://uscis.gov/graphics/services/residency/index.htm and Ruth Ellen Wasem, *U.S. Immigration Policy on Permanent Admissions,* CRS Report for Congress RL32235 (Congressional Research Service, February 18, 2004).

Note: LPR = lawful permanent resident.

a.   As defined by the Office of Immigration Statistics, refugees must apply for admission to the United States at an overseas facility and can enter only after their application is approved. Asylum-seekers apply for admission when already in the United States or at a point of entry.

b.   Parolees are those aliens deemed to be inadmissible by an inspecting officer but who are allowed to enter the United States for urgent humanitarian reasons or when an alien's entry would provide significant public benefit. Parole is an extraordinary measure that is granted on a case-by-case basis.

In 2004, about 50,000 refugee applications were approved, compared with a ceiling of 70,000.[9] For the same year, about 12,000 applications for refugee status were denied. Unlike refugee admissions, asylum admissions are not subject to an annual ceiling. In 2004, the USCIS approved about 10,000 applications for asylum, and an additional 11,000 people were granted asylum by the Executive Office for Immigration Review.[10]

Both refugees and asylum-seekers may file an application seeking lawful permanent resident status after one year in the United States. In 2004, about 71,000 LPR adjustments were granted to refugees and asylum-seekers, accounting for roughly 8 percent of all legal admissions to the United States. (At the time, LPR adjustments by asylum-seekers were subject to an annual limit but those of refugees were not.) In 2004, 10,000 asylum-seekers adjusted to LPR status. The Emergency Supplemental Appropriations Act for Defense, the Global War on Terror, and Tsunami Relief, 2005 (Public Law 109-13), eliminated the annual ceiling on LPR adjustments for asylum-seekers beginning in 2005.

9.   Department of Homeland Security, Office of Immigration Statistics, *2004 Yearbook of Immigration Statistics* (January 2006).

10.   Certain aliens may be granted asylum by the Executive Office for Immigration Review after USCIS places them in formal removal proceedings; those numbers are not reported in USCIS's count of asylum application approvals. See Department of Homeland Security, *2004 Yearbook of Immigration Statistics*; Department of Justice, Executive Office of Immigration Review, *Immigration Courts FY 2004 Asylum Statistics,* available at www.usdoj.gov/eoir/efoia/foiafreq.htm; and Government Accountability Office, *Immigration Statistics: Information Gaps, Quality Issues Limit Utility of Federal Data to Policymakers,* GAO-GGD-98-164 (July 1998).

Table 3.

Numerical Ceilings and Admissions, by Immigration Category, 2004

| Category | Total Ceiling | | Admissions[a] |
	Ceiling	Special Additions	
Immediate Relatives of U.S. Citizens	Not subject to ceiling		406,074
Family-Based Immigration[b]			
First preference: Unmarried adult (Ages 21 and older) sons and daughters of U.S. citizens	23,400	Plus visas not required for fourth preference	26,380
Second preference: Spouses and dependent children and unmarried sons and daughters of LPRs	114,200	Plus visas not required for first preference	93,609
Third preference: Married sons and daughters of U.S. citizens	23,400	Plus visas not required for first or second preference	28,695
Fourth preference: Siblings ages 21 and older of U.S. citizens	65,000	Plus visas not required for first, second, or third preference	65,671
Subtotal	**226,000**		**214,355**
Employment-Based Immigration			
First preference: Priority workers	58,465	Plus unused visas from fourth and fifth preference categories	31,291
Second preference: Members of the professions	58,465	Plus unused first preference visas	32,534
Third preference: Skilled and unskilled shortage workers	58,464	Plus unused visas from the first or second preference categories; 10,000 of these are reserved for unskilled workers	85,969
Fourth preference: Special immigrants	14,514		5,407
Fifth preference: Employment-creation investors	14,514		129
Subtotal	**204,422**		**155,330**

Continued

Diversity Program. The fourth goal of U.S. immigration policy is to provide admission for people from a diverse set of countries. Most of the nation's immigrants come from a small number of countries, largely because family reunification has been such an important facet of U.S. immigration policy. To increase immigration from countries with historically low immigration levels to the United States, the Immigration Act of 1990 introduced a new diversity-based admissions program. It provides another limited channel for immigrants to gain lawful entry into the country.

The diversity program has an annual ceiling of 50,000 visas; before 1999, the limit was 55,000 visas.[11] In 2004,

50,000 immigrants were admitted under this program, accounting for 5 percent of total legal immigration (see Table 4).

Immigrants from African and European countries have accounted for most of the immigrants admitted under the diversity program: 41 percent and 38 percent, respectively, in 2004. Under the family-based preference pro-

---

11. To accommodate visa issuances to certain immigrants under the Nicaraguan Adjustment and Central American Relief Act of 1997, the number of diversity-based visas available on an annual basis has been reduced by 5,000 since fiscal year 1999.

Table 3.

Continued

| Category | Total Ceiling | | Admissions[a] |
	Ceiling	Special Additions	
Diversity Program Participants	50,000		50,084
Asylum-Seekers[c]		No limit on receiving; limit of 10,000 on LPR adjustments[d]	10,016 [e]
Refugees[c]	70,000	Presidential determination; no limit on LPR adjustments	61,013 [e]
Other		Dependent on specific adjustment authority[f]	49,270
Total Overall Admissions	**N.A.**		**946,142**

Source: Congressional Budget Office based on Department of Homeland Security, Office of Immigration Statistics, *Annual Flow Report* (June 2005), and *2004 Yearbook of Immigration Statistics* (January 2006).

Note: LPR = lawful permanent resident; N.A. = not available

a.   This category includes both aliens who entered the United States as LPRs and those already present in the country who adjusted to LPR status in 2004. Thus, admissions may exceed ceilings.

b.   This category of preference immigrants does not include the immediate relatives of U.S. citizens, who are categorized as non preference immigrants and accounted for 406,074 admissions in 2004.

c.   Asylum-seekers and refugees are people who are unable or unwilling to return to their home country because of the risk of persecution or a well-founded fear of persecution. Refugees apply for admission from outside of the United States; asylum-seekers request legal admission from within the United States or at a U.S. port of entry.

d.   The Emergency Supplemental Appropriations Act for Defense, the Global War on Terror, and Tsunami Relief, 2005 (Public Law 109-13) eliminated the ceiling on LPR adjustments for asylum-seekers beginning in 2005.

e.   Asylum-seekers and refugees may apply for LPR status one year after being granted refugee status. The numbers shown here are for LPR adjustments of asylum-seekers and refugees. In addition, 10,101 asylum applications and 49,638 refugee admissions were approved.

f.   This category includes other immigrants (such as Amerasians, Cubans, and Haitians) who were granted adjustment to LPR status by specific legislation. The category also includes parolees, immigrants who appear to be inadmissible but are granted temporary admission for urgent humanitarian reasons or when admission is determined to be of significant public benefit.

grams, by contrast, the largest share of immigrants admitted in 2004 came from North America (including the Caribbean and Central America) and Asia (see Table 4).

Visas for the diversity program are issued through a lottery administered by the State Department. Eligible countries are sorted into six geographic regions, and visa limits are set for those regions on the basis of immigrant admissions in the past five years and a region's total population. Applicants must have either a high school diploma or its equivalent or two years of work experience within

the past five years. Countries that accounted for more than 50,000 immigrant admissions (under the numerically limited categories) during the previous five years are excluded from participation in the program.

Each year, the State Department randomly selects roughly 110,000 lottery applicants. Those who meet all of the requirements and complete the application process (not all do so) may be granted lawful permanent residency.

Table 4.

Immigrant Admissions Under the Diversity Program, by Region, 1997 to 2004

Region	1997	1998	1999	2000	2001	2002	2003	2004
All Countries	**49,374**	**45,499**	**47,571**	**50,945**	**42,015**	**42,829**	**46,347**	**50,084**
Europe	21,783	19,423	21,636	24,585	17,952	16,867	19,162	18,781
Africa	16,224	15,394	15,526	15,810	15,499	16,310	16,503	20,337
Asia	8,254	7,768	7,192	7,244	5,958	7,175	8,131	8,092
North America	1,387	1,298	1,474	1,226	728	589	394	471
South America	1,046	965	972	1,208	1,131	1,310	1,544	1,588
Caribbean	1,009	979	1,232	968	556	482	266	N.A.
Oceania	669	526	654	808	675	533	555	712
Central America	224	175	124	129	84	23	41	42

Source: Congressional Budget Office based on Department of Homeland Security, Office of Immigration Statistics, *2002 Yearbook of Immigration Statistics* (October 2003), *2003 Yearbook of Immigration Statistics* (September 2004), and *2004 Yearbook of Immigration Statistics* (January 2006); and Department of Justice, Immigration and Naturalization Service, *1997 Statistical Yearbook of the Immigration and Naturalization Service* (October 1999), *1998 Statistical Yearbook of the Immigration and Naturalization Service* (November 2000), *1999 Statistical Yearbook of the Immigration and Naturalization Service* (March 2002), *2000 Statistical Yearbook of the Immigration and Naturalization Service* (September 2002), and *2001 Statistical Yearbook of the Immigration and Naturalization Service* (February 2003).

Notes: N.A. = not available.

Some regional admissions may be undercounted.

Countries that do not qualify for the diversity program by world region:

- Asia—China (mainland and Taiwan; for 2002, also Macau, Hong Kong), India, Pakistan (disqualified for 2000 only), Philippines, South Korea, Vietnam;

- Europe—Great Britain and its territories, Poland (except in 1997, 2000, 2002);

- North America—Canada; and

- South and Central America and the Caribbean—Colombia, Dominican Republic, El Salvador, Haiti (except in 1997, 1998, and 1999), Jamaica, Mexico.

Temporary Admission

Nonimmigrants gain lawful admission temporarily for a specific purpose, such as tourism, study, business, temporary work, professional or cultural exchange, or diplomatic missions. According to preliminary data, in 2004 the United States issued almost 5 million nonimmigrant visas (see Figure 2). More than two-thirds of them were tourist, business, or border-crossing card/visitor combination visas (see Table 5).[12] Temporary worker, exchange visitor, and student visas were the next-largest groups that year, each accounting for roughly 5 percent of the total nonimmigrant visas issued.

Under the Visa Waiver Program, 15.8 million people were admitted in 2004 on a temporary basis.[13] Under that program, citizens of 27 participating countries may enter the United States without a visa for visits of 90 days or less.[14] Requirements are a machine-readable passport, compliance with admissions conditions during prior visits under the program, and no previous finding of ineligibility for a U.S. visa.

---

12. Department of State, Bureau of Consular Affairs, *Report of the Visa Office, 2003*, available at http://travel.state.gov/visa/about/report/report_2750.html. Includes all visitor (B) visas.

13. Department of Homeland Security, *2004 Yearbook of Immigration Statistics*, p. 77. That number may include multiple admissions by the same individual.

14. Countries taking part in the Visa Waiver Program as of May 2005 were Andorra, Australia, Austria, Belgium, Brunei, Denmark, Finland, France, Germany, Iceland, Ireland, Italy, Japan, Liechtenstein, Luxembourg, Monaco, the Netherlands, New Zealand, Norway, Portugal, San Marino, Singapore, Slovenia, Spain, Sweden, Switzerland, and the United Kingdom.

Figure 2.

Percentage of Nonimmigrant Visas Issued, by Visa Classification, 2003

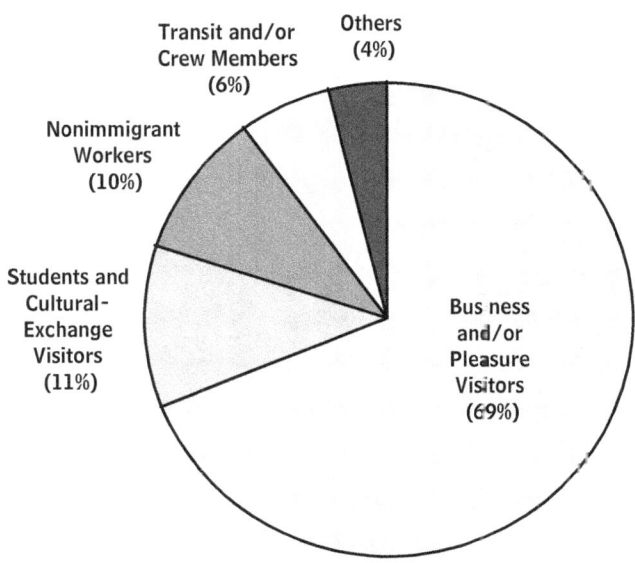

Source: Congressional Budget Office based on U.S. Department of State, Bureau of Consular Affairs, *Report of the Visa Office, 2003*, available at http://travel.state.gov/visa/about/report/report_2750.html.

Notes: The U.S. Citizenship and Immigration Services, a bureau of the Department of Homeland Security, defines a nonimmigrant as an alien who seeks temporary entry to the United States for a specific purpose.

A total of 4,881,632 nonimmigrant visas were issued in 2003 (the latest year for which data are available).

In general, anyone wishing to obtain a temporary visa must possess a valid passport and agree to abide by the terms of admission and to leave the United States at the end of the authorized stay. For most categories of temporary admission, applicants must keep a foreign residence and may be required to show proof of financial support.

H visas make up the largest category of nonimmigrant visas issued for employment; 287,000 workers received H visas in 2003. Various categories of H visas are numerically capped, subject to certain exemptions. Temporary workers entering the United States on H visas include specialty-occupation workers, registered nurses working in areas experiencing a shortage of health professionals, agricultural workers, and certain nonagricultural workers. Of the various subcategories of H visas, the largest is

H1-B, for temporary workers in professional specialities. Some 107,000 H1-B visas were issued in 2003.

The H category is a type of nonimmigrant visa that requires labor certification. Depending on the H visa subcategory, potential employers must either conduct an affirmative search for U.S. workers or attest that an immigrant worker's wages and working conditions will be comparable to those of a U.S. worker in a similar job.

Enforcement of Immigration Laws

The grounds for aliens' inadmissibility or removal include health concerns, criminal history, being identified as a security and terrorist risk, the likelihood of their becoming a public charge, their seeking work in the United States without proper labor certification and qualifications, prior illegal entry or immigration law violations, lack of proper documentation, ineligibility for citizenship, and previous removal from the country. The grounds for removal also include falsely claiming U.S. citizenship to obtain employment or receive a government benefit and conviction for a crime related to domestic violence, stalking, or child abuse.

Unauthorized Aliens

Unauthorized aliens include those who enter the United States without documentation or with forged documentation; lawfully admitted immigrants who remain in the United States after violating immigration law; and aliens who have entered the United States on a temporary visa and remained past the time limit of the visa.

The INS and Census Bureau estimated that, in 2000, the total number of unauthorized aliens in the United States was about 7 million. Another estimate based on survey data from the Current Population Survey and administrative data from DHS and other federal agencies estimated that 10 million unauthorized aliens were residing in the United States in early 2004.[15]

15. Immigration and Naturalization Services, Office of Policy and Planning, *Estimates of the Unauthorized Immigrant Population Residing in the United States: 1990 to 2000* (January 2003). Jeffrey S. Passel, "Unauthorized Migrants: Numbers and Characteristics," Background Briefing Prepared for Task Force on Immigration and America's Future, Pew Hispanic Center (June 14, 2005). The November 2004 CBO publication, *A Description of the Immigrant Population*, provides further details on the various methods used for estimating the unauthorized alien population in the United States.

Table 5.

Number and Type of Nonimmigrant (Temporary) Visa Issuances, 1992 to 2003

Type of Temporary Admission	Visa Class	1992	1993	1994	1995
Temporary Visitor (Excluding Visa Waiver Program)[a]					
Business	B-1	180,742	229,272	216,825	208,073
Pleasure	B-2	680,820	636,310	690,946	1,058,332
Business and pleasure	B-1/B-2	3,111,483	2,938,055	2,987,629	3,129,435
Combination B-1/B-2 and border-crossing card	B-1/B-2/BCC	299,075	429,436	532,611	543,122
Subtotal		4,272,120	4,233,073	4,428,011	4,938,962
Official Representative and Immediate Family	A,G	87,836	90,539	93,715	102,188
Transitional Family Member[b]	K	8,651	9,764	9,212	10,003
Student	F-1, M-1	223,309	215,756	219,941	233,840
Spouse or Child of Student	F-2, M-2	22,325	22,057	20,955	21,121
Subtotal		245,634	237,813	240,896	254,961
Intracompany Transferee[c]	L-1	17,345	20,369	22,666	29,088
Spouse or Child of Intracompany Transferee	L-2	21,358	23,832	26,450	33,508
Exchange Visitor	J-1	145,020	151,281	166,639	171,445
Spouse or Child of Exchange Visitor	J-2	32,470	33,360	32,151	33,481
Subtotal		177,490	184,641	198,790	204,926
NAFTA Professional	TN	d	d	4	34
Spouse or Child of NAFTA Professional	TD	d	d	18	114
Temporary Worker					
Registered nurse	H-1A	7,377	6,388	6,441	7,261
Worker of distinguished merit and ability	H-1B	44,290	35,818	42,843	51,832
Nurse in shortage area	H-1C	f	f	f	f
Worker in agricultural services	H-2A	6,445	7,243	7,721	8,379
Worker in other services	H-2B	12,552	9,691	10,400	11,737
Trainee	H-3	2,069	1,785	1,803	1,843
Spouse or child of temporary worker	H-4	24,756	25,432	28,800	33,318
Subtotal		97,489	86,357	98,008	114,370
Worker with Extraordinary Ability in Sciences, Arts, etc.	O-1, O-2	674	3,003	3,625	4,360
Internationally Recognized Athlete or Entertainer	P-1, P-2, P-3	4,319	15,060	19,938	23,208
Spouse or Child of Certain Foreign Worker	O-3, P-4	118	531	796	1,028
Cultural Exchange or Religious Worker	Q-1, Q-2, R-1	1,847	3,474	4,372	4,829
Spouse or Child of Cultural Exchange or Religious Worker	Q-3, R-2	320	630	988	1,021
Treaty Trader or Treaty Investor and Spouse and Children	E	31,805	30,563	30,931	30,185
International Media and Spouse and Children	I	9,463	9,379	14,698	11,698
Total[g]		**5,368,437**	**5,359,620**	**5,610,953**	**6,181,822**

Source: Congressional Budget Office based on Department of Homeland Security, Office of Immigration Statistics, *2003 Yearbook of Immigration Statistics* (September 2004); Alison Siskin, *Visa Waiver Program*, CRS Report for Congress RL32221 (Congressional Research Service, April 19, 2005); and Department of State, Bureau of Consular Affairs, *Report of the Visa Office, 1996* (April 1997), *Report of the Visa Office, 2000*, available at http://travel.state.gov/pdf/FY2000_TOC.pdf, and *Report of the Visa Office, 2003*, http://travel.state.gov/visa/about/report/report_2750.html.

Notes: Aliens issued a visa might not enter the United States in the year of issuance, as certain visas allow nonimmigrants to enter within a window of a few years.

      NAFTA = North American Free Trade Agreement.

a.   Under the Visa Waiver Program, the requirements for short-term B-visa visitors from certain countries are waived. As of May 2005, the program included Andorra, Australia, Austria, Belgium, Brunei, Denmark, Finland, France, Germany, Iceland, Ireland, Italy, Japan, Liechtenstein, Luxembourg, Monaco, the Netherlands, New Zealand, Norway, Portugal, San Marino, Singapore, Slovenia, Spain, Sweden, Switzerland, and the United Kingdom.

1996	1997	1998	1999	2000	2001	2002	2003
204,374	232,377	192,837	93,019	75,919	84,201	75,642	60,392
1,012,511	1,020,402	854,738	642,676	509,031	381,431	255,487	271,358
3,369,635	3,070,539	3,226,799	3,447,822	3,567,580	3,527,118	2,528,103	2,207,303
361,379	387,845	289,883	676,386	1,510,133	1,990,402	1,399,819	836,407
4,947,899	4,711,163	4,564,257	4,859,903	5,662,663	5,983,152	4,259,051	3,375,960
108,336	108,512	110,396	111,971	117,609	111,165	117,155	114,606
11,597	13,455	14,467	19,456	24,746	28,712	39,008	44,633
247,432	273,558	258,080	268,782	290,160	298,730	238,438	219,852
21,518	22,383	22,302	23,230	25,339	26,445	22,373	20,029
268,950	295,941	280,382	292,012	315,499	325,175	260,811	239,881
32,098	36,589	38,307	41,739	54,963	59,384	57,721	57,245
37,617	43,476	44,176	46,289	57,069	61,154	54,903	53,571
171,164	179,598	192,451	211,349	236,837	261,769	253,841	253,866
33,068	34,089	33,177	34,394	37,122	38,189	32,539	29,796
204,232	213,687	225,628	245,743	273,959	299,958	286,380	233,662
115	171	295	484	906	787	699	423
231	340	530	704	1,128	1,041	856	796
1,745	61	18	5	2	e	e	e
58,327	80,547	91,360	116,513	133,290	161,643	118,352	107,196
f	f	f	f	f	34	212	191
11,004	16,011	22,676	28,568	30,201	31,523	31,538	29,882
12,200	15,706	20,192	30,642	45,037	58,215	62,591	78,955
1,877	1,747	1,830	1,892	1,514	1,613	1,387	1,417
36,187	47,206	54,595	69,194	79,518	95,967	79,725	69,289
121,340	161,278	190,671	246,814	289,562	348,995	293,805	286,930
4,359	5,193	6,035	7,194	8,360	8,584	7,998	8,598
23,885	26,941	30,064	30,572	34,525	32,998	32,537	33,463
1,083	1,355	1,684	2,222	2,969	3,307	2,698	2,447
5,946	6,372	6,762	8,333	9,800	10,121	10,444	10,604
1,226	1,291	1,395	2,003	2,492	3,195	3,176	3,164
29,909	29,758	30,232	32,948	36,520	36,886	33,444	32,096
21,494	12,056	11,627	12,694	13,928	13,799	18,187	12,329
6,237,870	5,942,061	5,814,153	6,192,478	7,141,636	7,588,778	5,769,437	4,881,632

b.   Includes fiance(e)s of U.S. citizens and their children, and spouses of U.S. citizens awaiting the availability of a permanent visa.

c.   Includes executive, managerial, and specialized personnel continuing their employment with an international firm or corporation.

d.   Section 341 of the North American Free Trade Agreement Implementation Act (Public Law 103-182), enacted on December 8, 1993, established this visa category.

e.   Section 2(c) of the Nursing Relief for Disadvantaged Areas Act of 1999 (P.L. 106-95) repealed this visa category.

f.   Section 2(a) of the Nursing Relief for Disadvantaged Areas Act of 1999 (P.L. 106-95) established this visa category, which was in effect from June 11, 2001, through June 11, 2005.

g.   Categories may not sum to totals because of certain omitted categories.

According to USCIS, about one-third had violated the time limits of their temporary visas, thus rendering those visas invalid.[16] However, some studies indicate that USCIS has underestimated the proportion of illegal aliens that violated the time limits of their temporary visas, or overstay. For example, a Government Accountability Office report found that the USCIS estimate of "overstayers" did not include Canadian citizens, certain Mexican citizens who enter the United States with a border-crossing card, and other short-term overstayers.[17]

Enforcement Procedures

Apprehensions are the arrest of aliens found to be in violation of immigration law. In 2000, apprehensions were at a high of 1.8 million; however, by 2002, apprehensions had dropped to 1.0 million (see Table 6). According to USCIS, apprehensions made along the southwest border between the United States and Mexico accounted for over 98 percent of all apprehensions made by the Border Patrol. Apprehensions along the U.S. border with Mexico, as compared with other Border Patrol sectors, accounted for the greatest decline in total apprehensions for the years 2001 through 2003; it is uncertain what factors may have contributed to that decline.[18] In 2004, approximately 1.2 million aliens were apprehended; the Border Patrol made 93 percent of those apprehensions.[19]

Aliens apprehended and found in violation of U.S. immigration laws may be removed from the country through formal removal or a voluntary departure. Formal removal proceedings are conducted before an immigration judge and may result in the removal of the alien or an adjust-

ment of immigration status. Penalties associated with formal removal may include fines, imprisonment, and prohibition of future legal entry. Under some circumstances, including a history of legal residence in the country or the presence of dependent family in the United States, the court may allow the alien to remain in the United States.

An expedited removal process was introduced in 1997, applicable to aliens attempting to enter the country illegally. In an expedited removal, the arriving alien may be removed without further hearing or review if it is determined that the alien is inadmissible because of fraud, misrepresentation, or lack of proper documentation.

Noncriminal, unauthorized aliens attempting entry may be offered voluntary departure in lieu of formal removal. Aliens who are allowed to depart voluntarily must admit that they were in the country illegally and agree to a witnessed departure, but they are not barred from seeking legal admission at a later time.

Over the past two decades, the number of formal removals of aliens has generally increased. From 1981 to 1990, formal removals averaged 23,300; from 1991 to 2000, they averaged 94,000.[20] However, formal removals decreased for 2001 and 2002.[21] USCIS suggests that increased border security after September 11, 2001, may have deterred some immigrants from entering the country illegally, which resulted in fewer removals. However, some researchers have suggested that more illegal immigrants are staying longer in the United States, thus resulting in fewer attempted illegal entries and fewer removals.[22] In 2004, there were about 203,000 formal removals; 42,000 unauthorized immigrants were subject to expedited removals; and 1 million unauthorized immigrants departed voluntarily (see Table 6).

16. Department of Homeland Security, Office of Immigration Statistics, *2002 Yearbook of Immigration Statistics* (October 2003).

17. Government Accountability Office, *Overstay Trackings: A Key Component of Homeland Security and a Layered Defense*, GAO-04-82 (May 2004).

18. Department of Homeland Security, Office of Immigration Statistics, *2003 Yearbook of Immigration Statistics* (September 2004), pp. 146 and 155.

19. Department of Homeland Security, *2004 Yearbook of Immigration Statistics*. According to the *2003 Yearbook of Immigration Statistics* (p. 146), immigration inspectors technically do not apprehend aliens, which is the responsibility of the Border Patrol. The remaining apprehensions were administrative apprehensions made by Immigration and Customs Enforcement.

20. Department of Homeland Security, *2003 Yearbook of Immigration Statistics*, p. 158.

21. Department of Homeland Security, *2002 Yearbook of Immigration Statistics*, p. 176; and Department of Justice, Immigration and Naturalization Service, *2001 Statistical Yearbook of the Immigration and Naturalization Service* (February 2003), p. 235.

22. Belinda I. Reyes, Hans P. Johnson, and Richard Van Swearingen, *Holding the Line? The Effect of Recent Border Build-Up on Unauthorized Immigration* (San Francisco: Public Policy Institute of California, July 2002).

Table 6.

Enforcement Efforts, 1991 to 2004

	Apprehensions[a]	Formal Removals			Voluntary Departures[d]
		Nonexpedited	Expedited[b]	Total[c]	
1991	1,197,875	33,189	n.a.	33,189	1,061,105
1992	1,258,481	43,671	n.a.	43,671	1,105,829
1993	1,327,261	42,542	n.a.	42,542	1,243,410
1994	1,094,719	45,674	n.a.	45,674	1,029,107
1995	1,394,554	50,924	n.a.	50,924	1,313,764
1996	1,649,986	69,680	n.a.	69,680	1,573,428
1997	1,536,520	91,190	23,242	114,432	1,440,684
1998	1,679,439	97,068	76,078	173,146	1,570,127
1999	1,714,035	91,902	89,170	181,072	1,574,682
2000	1,814,729	100,296	85,926	186,222	1,675,711
2001	1,387,486	108,185	69,841	178,026	1,254,035
2002	1,062,279	116,006	34,536	150,542	934,119
2003	1,046,422	145,610	43,758	189,368	887,115
2004	1,241,089	161,090	41,752	202,842	1,035,477

Source: Congressional Budget Office based on Department of Homeland Security, Office of Immigration Statistics, *Annual Report: Immigration Enforcement Actions: 2004* (November 2005), and *2004 Yearbook of Immigration Statistics* (January 2006).

Notes: The sum of all formal removals and voluntary departures may not equal total apprehensions for various reasons. Formal removal proceedings for some apprehended aliens may take months or several years to resolve; other apprehended aliens may be granted an adjustment of status following an immigration hearing; some aliens may be apprehended and removed or may voluntarily depart more than once.

   n.a. = not applicable.

a. Apprehensions represent the arrest of removable immigrants.

b. Expedited removals are a type of formal removal introduced in 1997. Expedited removal allows an immigration officer to remove an arriving immigrant without further hearing or review if it is determined that the immigrant is inadmissible because of fraud, misrepresentation, or lack of proper documentation.

c. Formal removals include all forms of removal (of unauthorized immigrants, for inadmissibility, and for violation of immigration law) except voluntary departures.

d. Immigrants allowed to voluntarily depart admit that they were in the country illegally and must agree to a witnessed departure. These immigrants are not barred from seeking lawful admission at a later time.

The types of formal removal charges, or the administrative reasons for formal removal, have changed over the past decade (see Table 7). Before 1997, aliens removed for criminal reasons accounted for the largest share of aliens removed. However, between 1998 and 2001, aliens attempting entry without proper documents accounted for the largest share of aliens removed. From 2002 to 2004, aliens present in the United States without authorization made up the largest percentage of aliens removed.[23]

---

23. Department of Homeland Security, *2004 Yearbook of Immigration Statistics.*

Table 7.

Administrative Reasons for Formal Removal, 1991 to 2004

	1991	1992	1993	1994	1995	1996	1997	1998	1999	2000	2001	2002	2003	2004
	Thousands of Removals													
Attempted Entry Without Proper Documents	3	4	3	3	6	15	36	79	92	90	76	41	53	50
Criminal	14	20	22	25	26	28	34	36	42	41	40	38	40	43
Failed to Maintain Status	1	1	1	1	1	1	1	1	1	1	1	1	1	1
Previously Removed, Ineligible for Reentry	1	1	1	1	1	2	3	7	9	12	11	13	18	20
Present Without Authorization	13	17	15	16	17	24	39	48	35	40	48	56	75	86
Security	*	*	*	*	*	*	*	*	*	*	*	*	*	*
Smuggling or Aiding Illegal Entry	*	*	*	*	*	*	*	*	*	*	1	1	1	1
Other	*	*	*	*	*	*	1	1	2	2	2	1	1	3
Total	**33**	**44**	**43**	**46**	**51**	**70**	**114**	**173**	**181**	**186**	**178**	**151**	**189**	**203**
	Percentage of Yearly Total													
Attempted Entry Without Proper Documents	9	8	7	8	11	22	31	46	51	48	43	27	28	25
Criminal	44	46	53	54	50	40	30	21	23	22	23	25	21	21
Failed to Maintain Status	3	2	2	2	1	1	1	1	*	*	*	1	1	1
Previously Removed, Ineligible for Reentry	2	2	2	2	3	3	3	4	5	6	6	9	9	10
Present Without Authorization	40	40	35	34	34	34	34	28	19	22	27	37	40	42
Security	*	*	*	*	*	*	*	*	*	*	*	*	*	*
Smuggling or Aiding Illegal Entry	*	*	*	*	*	*	*	*	*	*	*	*	*	*
Other	*	*	*	*	*	*	*	*	1	1	1	1	1	1
Total	**100**	**100**	**100**	**100**	**100**	**100**	**100**	**100**	**100**	**100**	**100**	**100**	**100**	**100**

Source: Congressional Budget Office based on Department of Homeland Security, Office of Immigration Statistics, *2004 Yearbook of Immigration Statistics* (January 2006), and *2003 Yearbook of Immigration Statistics* (September 2004).

Note: * = fewer than 500 or less than 0.5 percent.

Appendix: Becoming a U.S. Citizen

Naturalization is the process by which an immigrant can attain U.S. citizenship. In general, any lawful permanent resident who has maintained a period of continuous residence and presence in the United States can apply for naturalization. Applicants for naturalization must have good moral character, knowledge of U.S. history and government and the English language, and a willingness to support and defend the United States and its Constitution. Most immigrants may apply for naturalization after three to five years of permanent residency. For certain groups of immigrants, including those who have served in the U.S. military, the requirements for permanent residency may be shortened or waived. The requirements for U.S. residency and local residency also vary according to the circumstances of the immigrant. (Table A-1 details the requirements for naturalization for various categories of immigrants.)

In 2004, U.S. citizenship was conferred upon 537,000 individuals through naturalization. That represents an increase in the annual number of naturalizations, which had declined since 2000 when 889,000 persons were naturalized. According to the Department of Homeland Security, yearly naturalization levels reflect levels of legal immigration; typically, the number of yearly naturalizations lags behind legal immigration levels by six to seven years. However, because of processing backlogs, naturalization numbers may not accurately reflect demand for citizenship among lawful permanent residents.

Table A-1.

Requirements for Naturalization

| Characteristics of Applicant | Preconditions | | | |
	Time as Lawful Permanent Resident	Continuous Residence in the United States[a]	Physical Presence in the United States	Time in District/State[b]
Lawful Permanent Residents with No Special Circumstances	Five years	Five years	30 months	Three months
Married to and Living with a U.S. Citizen for the Past Three Years; Spouse Must Have Been a Citizen for the Past Three Years	Three years	Three years	18 months	Three months
In the Armed Forces for at Least One Year	Must be an LPR at the time of interview	Not required	Not required	Not required
In the Armed Forces for Less than One Year, or in the Armed Forces Less than One Year and Discharged More than Six Months Earlier	Five years	Five years	30 months	Three months
Performed Active Military Duty During World War I, World War II, Korea, Vietnam, Persian Gulf, on or After September 11, 2001	Not required	Not required	Not required	Not required
Widow or Widower of a U.S. Citizen Who Died During Active Duty	Must be an LPR at the time of interview	Not required	Not required	Not required
Employee of, or Under Contract to, U.S. Government	Five years	Five years	30 months	Three months
Performing Ministerial or Priestly Functions for a Religious Denomination or an Interdenominational Organization with a Valid U.S. Presence	Five years	Five years	30 months	Three months

Continued

Table A-1.

Continued

Characteristics of Applicant	Preconditions			
	Time as Lawful Permanent Resident	Continuous Residence in the United States[a]	Physical Presence in the United States	Time in District/State[b]
Employed by Certain U.S. Research Institutions, a U.S.-Owned Firm Involved with Development of U.S. Foreign Trade or Commerce, or Public International Organizations of Which the United States Is a Member	Five years	Five years	30 months	Three months
Employed for Five Years or More by a U.S. Nonprofit Organization Supporting U.S. Interests Abroad Through Communications Media	Five years	Not required	Not required	Not required
Spouse of a U.S. Citizen Who Is a Member of the Armed Forces, or in One of the Four Previous Categories, and Who Is Working Abroad Under an Employment Contract with a Qualifying Employer for at Least One Year (Including the Time at Which the Applicant Naturalizes)	Must be an LPR at the time of interview	Not required	Not required	Not required

Source: Congressional Budget Office based on Department of Homeland Security, U.S. Citizenship and Immigration Services, *A Guide to Naturalization* (February 2004).

Note: LPR = lawful permanent resident.

Applicants also must demonstrate good moral character, knowledge of civics and the English language, and "an attachment to the U.S. Constitution."

a.   Trips outside of the United States for periods of six months or longer constitute a break in continuous U.S. residency. Exceptions are made for members of the Armed Forces whose service takes them out of the country.

b.   Most applicants must be a resident of the district or state in which they are applying.

Page Intentionally Left Blank

Page Intentionally Left Blank

Page Intentionally Left Blank

Page Intentionally Left Blank

INSIDE MAIL